T0194904

When DADDY Could Make It BETTER

Jeremy Stinson

³ Children are a heritage from the LORD,
    offspring a reward from him.
⁴ Like arrows in the hands of a warrior
    are children born in one's youth.
⁵ Blessed is the man
    whose quiver is full of them.
  They will not be put to shame
    when they contend with their opponents in court.

Psalms 127:3-5, NIV

WestBow Press books may be ordered through booksellers or by contacting:

WestBow Press
A Division of Thomas Nelson & Zondervan
1663 Liberty Drive
Bloomington, IN 47403
www.westbowpress.com
1 (866) 928-1240

ISBN: 978-1-9736-3619-9 (sc)
ISBN: 978-1-9736-3620-5 (e)

Library of Congress Control Number: 2018909254

Print information available on the last page.

WestBow Press rev. date: 9/13/2018

WESTBOW
PRESS®
A DIVISION OF THOMAS NELSON
& ZONDERVAN

When you were a baby and needed me, Daddy could make it better.

Daddy could hold you.

Daddy could rock you.

Daddy could give you a bottle.

Daddy could change
your diaper,

And Daddy loved you.

When you were learning to walk and needed me, Daddy could make it better.

Daddy would
hold your hand.

**Daddy would kiss
your boo-boos.**

Daddy made sure you
had your water cup.

Daddy would help you eat,

And Daddy loved you.

When you started school you still needed me, and Daddy tried to make it better.

Daddy worried about not being able to hold your hand.

Daddy worried about you getting boo-boos and him not being there.

**Daddy worried you would be thirsty,
and not have your water cup.**

Daddy worried he would not be there to help you,

And Daddy loved you.

While you may think me your hero, I cannot make everything better.

Things change, but Daddy's love can never go away.

Some weeks we are three, and some weeks it is just me.

Nothing you did made this bad thing happen.

Daddy loves you, and that will never, ever change.

What we can do is pray, that God will make things better.

You and I know we are together
even when we are apart.

You know I am here when you need me.

You are Daddy's heart.

And Daddy loves you.

Printed in the United States
By Bookmasters